Wealthy Habits: Financial Success for the Millennial Generation

A Millennial's Guide to Financial Freedom

Bailey Hodgson

Table of Contents

Introduction

Understanding Millennial Financial Challenges

Millennials, often referred to as the generation born between the early 1980s and the mid-1990s, face unique financial challenges shaped by the evolving economic and social landscape of our time. In the dynamic landscape of the 21st century, millennials navigate a complex web of financial issues that require a nuanced understanding and a strategic approach. As a guide on this journey, let's delve into the complexities of these challenges to understand and build the knowledge needed for financial mastery.

1. ***Student Loans Struggle:*** One thing many millennials have in common is the burden of student loans. The

pursuit of higher education, while transformative, often leaves graduates with substantial debt. From repayment plans to strategically handling loan forgiveness programs, understanding the intricacies of student loan management is essential.

2. ***Housing Dilemmas:*** With real estate prices on the rise, the dreams of homeownership may feel like a distant mirage. Millennials are challenged by the reality of balancing housing aspirations with financial prudence. Exploring alternatives such as shared ownership, innovative financing, or strategic leasing options becomes important in these housing challenges.

3. ***Gig Economy Realities:*** The gig economy has ushered in a new era of work flexibility, but it also comes with

its challenges. Income instability and erratic cash flow require a change in mindset. Embracing the gig economy requires not only adaptation but also a focus on financial stability through multiple income streams and prudent budgeting.

4. ***Technological Influences***: Living in a digitally interconnected world brings both unprecedented convenience and potential risks. The continued appeal of online transactions and the impact of social media on spending patterns pose challenges for financial discipline. Using technology as a tool for financial growth while mastering the art of resisting impulsive digital temptations is an essential skill

5. **Retirement Uncertainty:** The traditional retirement journey is

changing, and millennials are at the forefront of this paradigm shift. Building a vision for retirement in the face of changing work structures, pension uncertainties, and evolving expectations requires a strategic approach to long-term financial planning.

6. ***Economic volatility***: Millennials have weathered economic storms, from the aftermath of the global financial crisis to recent global events. These experiences have led to a cautious and risk-aware approach to financial decision-making. Managing economic uncertainties requires a blend of financial literacy, adaptive strategies, and a sustainable financial mindset.

Understanding these multifaceted challenges is not just a theoretical exercise; it is the basis for developing a sustainable financial strategy. By addressing each challenge with insight, millennials can turn what appear to be financial obstacles into stepping stones to financial well-being and future prosperity. Remember that every challenge is an opportunity in disguise, and with the right guidance, you can confidently navigate your way to financial success.

The Importance of Wealthy Habits

The common thread that weaves everything together in the grand tapestry of financial well-being is cultivating wealth habits. Think of these habits not just as routines but as the foundation of lasting financial success. As your guide on this journey of transformation, let's discover the deeper meaning of developing and cultivating these habits.

- **Foundation of Financial Stability:** Wealthy habits are the foundation of financial security. By establishing routines like budgeting, tracking expenses, and consistent savings, people build a solid foundation to protect themselves from unexpected financial storms. These habits serve as your financial compass and give you direction despite uncertainty.

- **Power of Compound Growth:** At the heart of wealthy habits is the power of compound growth. Steady savings and smart investing combine over time to grow your wealth exponentially. By understanding and harnessing these financial forces, people can witness the snowball effect of disciplined effort.

- **Stress Reduction and Peace of Mind:** Financial stress can cast a heavy shadow over all aspects of life. Wealthy habits act as a shield against this stress, creating a sense of control and order. When people feel in control of their financial destiny through habits like saving an emergency fund and debt management, their mental well-being and peace of mind are enhanced.

- **Goal Achievement and Aspirations:** Each financial journey is uniquely personal, woven with individual dreams and ambitions. Wealthy habits motivate people to achieve these goals. Whether you're buying a home, starting a business, or enjoying a comfortable retirement, these habits provide a roadmap for turning your aspirations into tangible accomplishments.

- **Adaptive Financial Resilience:** The financial environment is dynamic and subject to economic changes and unexpected challenges. Wealthy habits build adaptive financial resilience. People with these habits are better positioned to handle economic uncertainties, job changes, and unexpected expenses, becoming stronger and more resilient.

- **Generational Wealth Creation:** Wealthy habits transcend individual lifetimes; they have the power to create a lasting legacy. By passing on these habits from generation to generation, individuals contribute to the creation of sustainable family wealth. This legacy goes beyond monetary assets and includes the wisdom and knowledge needed to navigate the financial landscape successfully.

- **Freedom to Pursue Passions:** Ultimately, wealthy habits lead to financial freedom. Whether it's the freedom to pursue passions, take advantage of new opportunities, or enjoy life without financial constraints, these habits unlock the doors to a life rich in experiences and possibilities.

In the grand symphony of financial success, wealthy habits play the tune that orchestrates a harmonious and fulfilling life. As you begin this journey of transformation, remember that developing these habits isn't just about accumulating wealth; it's about creating abundance, security, and the freedom to live life on your terms.

Setting the Foundation

Defining Financial Goals

In the intricate tapestry of financial well-being, defining clear and meaningful financial goals serves as the compass that guides us on a purposeful journey. As your guide on this voyage of financial self-discovery, let's look at the profound significance of setting and defining financial goals.

1. *Visionary Blueprint for Success:*
Financial goals are more than numbers on a balance sheet; they are visionary blueprints that will guide you on your way to success. By defining your ambitions (whether it's home ownership, travel, education, or retirement), you can create a road map that turns your dreams into realistic and achievable milestones.

2. *Clarity Amidst Financial Noise:*

In a world full of financial information and options, defining your financial goals can provide clarity amidst the noise. It acts as a filter, helping you distinguish between what truly aligns with your ambitions and what may be distracting you from your financial journey.

3. *Motivation and Purpose:*

Financial goals are the key to motivation. They infuse purpose into your financial endeavors, transforming routine actions like budgeting and saving into intentional steps toward a greater purpose. When you face challenges, your goals become the driving force propelling you forward.

4. *Tailored to your Unique Journey:*

Your financial journey is as unique as your fingerprint. Setting financial goals helps you align your journey with your values, priorities, and schedule. It's not about following a set pattern; it's about creating a financial narrative that resonates with your ambitions and lifestyle.

5. *Empowerment through Milestones:*

Setting incremental milestones within your financial goals can help you feel a sense of accomplishment along the way. Celebrating these small victories motivates you to continue your journey and reinforces your belief that your financial dreams are an achievable goal and not a distant star.

6. *Financial Security and Peace of Mind:*

Financial goals serve as guardians of your financial stability. Whether it's an emergency fund, insurance coverage, or debt reduction, these goals provide peace of mind and build a financial safety net that allows you to confidently navigate uncertainties.

7. *Adaptability for Life Changes:*

Life is dynamic, and so are your financial needs. Defined financial goals are adaptable to life changes. You can keep your goals relevant and achievable by adjusting them to changing circumstances, such as changing jobs, starting a family, or unexpected expenses.

8. *Generational Legacy and Impact:*

Beyond personal accomplishments, financial goals have the potential to create a long-term legacy. By instilling financial wisdom and goal-setting habits, you can impact generations, creating a legacy of financial empowerment that will last a lifetime.

Defining your financial goals in the great tapestry of financial success is not a one-time task but an ever-evolving process. This is an effort to understand that self-discovery, empowerment, and financial journeys are not just about numbers; it's about creating a life that aligns with your deepest ambitions and values. Remember, every goal you set is a step towards the financial achievements that will make your dreams come true.

Creating a Budget that Works

Starting your financial wellness journey is like setting sail on a sea of possibilities. As your experienced guide, I am here to highlight important navigation tools for this expedition. This means creating a budget that not only works but also serves as a powerful tool for financial empowerment.

- ☐ **The Foundation of Financial Mastery:** Basically, a budget is the foundation of financial mastery. This is not just a table of numbers; it is a strategic plan that empowers you to take control of your financial destiny. Budgeting lays the foundation for making informed decisions, spending responsibly, and, most importantly, achieving your financial goals.

☐ **Understanding your Financial Landscape:** Effective budgeting starts with a deep understanding of your financial situation. It is a reflective process where you evaluate your income, expenses, debts, and financial goals. Understanding your financial intricacies will give you the foundation to create a budget that is not only functional but tailored to your unique situation.

☐ **Setting Realistic Goals and Priorities:** A successful budget is based on reality. It's about setting goals that are achievable and aligned with your priorities. Whether it's saving for a down payment, paying off debt, or building an emergency fund, your budget becomes a road map that guides you toward those goals.

☐ **Categorizing and Prioritizing Expenses:** A well-structured budget categorizes and prioritizes expenses. Essentials such as housing, utilities, and food come first, followed by discretionary spending. This careful categorization ensures that your budget reflects your core needs and values.

☐ **Embracing Flexibility:** Life is dynamic, and so should be your budget. A rigid budget can often lead to frustration. Instead, develop a budget that embraces flexibility. Be prepared for unexpected expenses, allow for adjustments, and recognize that occasional indulgences are part of a balanced financial life.

☐ **Build an Emergency Fund:** One of the keys to a sustainable budget is including an emergency fund. Life is unpredictable, and a financial safety net protects you from the unexpected. This fund provides peace of mind, allowing you to face challenges with confidence.

☐ **Tracking and Adjusting**: Budgeting is an ongoing process, not a one-time task. Regularly track your spending against your budget and be prepared to make adjustments if necessary. This iterative approach ensures that the budget remains a dynamic tool that evolves as circumstances change.

☐ **Cultivating Financial Discipline:** A budget is not just about numbers; it's about cultivating financial discipline. This will help you make informed choices, reduce impulse spending, and focus on your financial goals. This discipline becomes the cornerstone of your journey to financial empowerment.

Remember, budgeting is a liberating action, not a restrictive one; It is the key to unlocking financial freedom, allowing you to deploy your resources wisely and steer your financial ship to the shores of your ambitions. As your guide on this journey, I encourage you to look at your budget not as a constraint but as a powerful tool to create the financial life of your dreams.

Mastering Money Mindset

Overcoming Financial Mind Blocks

In the complex realm of financial well-being, the mind plays a central role as both a navigator and an occasional stumbling block. As your experienced guide on this transformational journey, we'll take a closer look at the profound subject of overcoming financial mind blocks—the subtle obstacles that, when dismantled, open the door to true financial empowerment.

- ***Unmasking Limiting Beliefs:*** Financial mind blocks often stem from deep-seated limiting beliefs about money. This can manifest as ideas, societal expectations, or experiences inherited from childhood that have shaped your view of financial success. The first step to overcoming these obstacles is recognizing and releasing these limiting beliefs.

- ***Fear of Scarcity:*** A common mental block is the fear of scarcity -the constant worry that there won't be enough. These fears can lead to hoarding money, investment avoidance, or reluctance to spend money on important needs. Overcoming this obstacle requires cultivating an abundant mindset and the recognition that opportunities for financial growth are abundant and attainable.

- ***Guilt and Shame Around Money:*** Feelings of guilt or shame related to money can be powerful mind blocks. Whether they stem from past financial mistakes or public opinions, it's important to release these feelings. Realizing that financial setbacks are learning experiences rather than an expression of personal worth is key to overcoming this block.

- ***Imposter Syndrome in Finances:*** Imposter syndrome can cause financial problems due to feelings of inadequacy despite apparent success. Individuals may question their ability to manage their wealth or make sound financial decisions. Overcoming these obstacles requires recognizing your accomplishments, seeking financial education, and developing confidence in your ability to navigate your financial journey.

- ***Procrastination and Financial Inertia:*** Procrastination often manifests as a mind block when it comes to financial matters. Delaying budgeting, investments, or paying off debt because you feel overwhelmed or avoidance can hinder financial progress. To overcome these obstacles, set manageable goals, take small steps, and recognize that imperfect action is better than no action.

- **Fear of Investing**: Fear of investing due to concerns about market volatility or lack of understanding can hinder your opportunities to build wealth. Overcoming this hurdle requires financial education, seeking professional advice, and understanding that investing is a gradual, long-term strategy.

- **Self-Worth and Financial Success**: A person's self-esteem can have a significant impact on their financial mindset. Believing that you are not worthy of financial success can create a powerful barrier. Overcoming this requires a shift in perspective, an awareness of intrinsic value, and an understanding that financial success can be achieved through intentional effort.

- ***Cultivating a Positive Financial Mindset:*** Ultimately, to overcome financial mindset barriers, you need to develop a positive financial mindset. This includes reframing negative thoughts, visualizing financial success, and surrounding yourself with positive financial influences. Constantly affirming your ability to overcome financial challenges can change the way you think about opportunities.

Remember, overcoming financial mind blocks doesn't happen overnight. It is an ongoing journey of self-awareness, conscious transformation, and intentional action. As your guide, I encourage you to begin this journey with patience, self-compassion, and the understanding that overcoming these obstacles in your mind is a powerful step toward realizing your full financial potential.

Cultivating a Positive Money Mindset

In the intricate dance of financial well-being, the mind is both a powerful architect and a subtle destroyer. Developing a positive attitude towards money is not just a financial strategy; it's a fundamental shift in your relationship with money that can determine the trajectory of your financial journey. As your trusted guide, let's explore the revolutionary process for fostering a positive money mindset.

1. **Awareness of Money Scripts:**

Begin this journey by untangling the intricate web of money scripts—the deep-seated beliefs about money that have accumulated over the years. These scripts, often inherited from family, culture, or past experiences, determine your attitudes and behavior. Awareness is the first step to understanding these scenarios and turning them into positive narratives.

2. Embracing an Abundance Mentality:
At the heart of a positive mindset towards money is an abundance mentality—an unwavering belief that there are many opportunities for financial growth, success, and prosperity. Instead of looking at life from a perspective of scarcity, focus on the endless possibilities that financial abundance can bring.

3. Gratitude as a Catalyst:

Gratitude serves as a potent catalyst for a positive money mindset. Regardless of your size, take the time to evaluate your financial achievements. Recognize the lessons you've learned from your financial struggles and be grateful for the present moment. This experience will bring enrichment and satisfaction to your financial journey.

4. Reframing Negative Thoughts:
Negative thoughts about money can act as a powerful obstacle. Challenge these thoughts and turn them into positive and powerful narratives. For example, replace your thoughts about financial hardship with opportunities for growth and learning. This shift in perspective can make all the difference in developing a positive money mindset.

5. Mindful Spending and Saving:
Conscious and deliberate spending and saving practices contribute significantly to a

positive money mindset. Align your spending with your values and make sure every financial decision reflects your priorities. Mindful saving reinforces the idea that you're actively building a foundation for future financial security and freedom.

6. Visualization and Manifestation Techniques:

Visualizing your financial goals and success can be a powerful tool in shaping your mindset about money. Create a vivid mental image of achieving your financial ambitions. Use manifestation techniques to strengthen positive beliefs about money, inviting prosperity into your life.

7. Surrounding Yourself with Positivity:

Your environment significantly influences your mindset. Surround yourself with positive financial influences, such as books, mentors, and communities that uplift and inspire. Engage in conversations that promote financial empowerment and seek out resources that strengthen a healthy perspective about money.

8. Affirmations on Financial Empowerment:

Incorporate positive affirmations into your daily routine to rewire your subconscious mind. Affirmations such as "I am financially empowered" or "I attract abundance into my life" will help you gradually change your mindset and develop a positive and confident attitude towards your financial journey.

Developing a positive attitude toward money is a journey of self-awareness and intentional choices. This requires patience, self-compassion, and a desire for personal growth. As your guide on this journey of transformation, I encourage you to embrace the power of your thoughts as you open the door to a future where financial abundance and well-being are not just aspirations but realities.

Debt Demolition

Strategies for Paying Down Debt

Embarking on the journey to financial freedom involves navigating the terrain of debt with purpose and strategy. As your expert guide, we'll walk you through a comprehensive set of strategies to help you pay off your debt and regain control of your financial records.

- ☐ ***Face the Numbers with Courage:*** The first step in overcoming debt is to face the numbers with courage and openness. Make a detailed list of all your debts, including amounts owed, interest rates, and minimum monthly payments. This realistic assessment is the basis for creating an effective debt repayment strategy.

☐ ***Prioritize and Strategize***: Not all debts are created equal. Prioritize your debts based on interest rates, paying attention to the highest interest rates first. Allocate additional funds to high-interest loans while maintaining minimum payments on all loans. This strategic approach minimizes the overall interest paid and accelerates the path to debt freedom.

☐ ***Create a Realistic Budget:*** Preparing a realistic budget is key to paying off debt effectively. Identify areas where expenses can be trimmed, and allocate the surplus towards debt repayment. A budget serves as a guiding framework to ensure that every dollar has a purpose on your path to financial recovery.

☐ ***Embrace the Debt Snowball Method:*** The debt snowball method, popularized by financial expert Dave Ramsey, involves paying off the smallest debts first and keeping minimum payments on larger debts. As smaller debts are paid off, momentum builds, providing psychological victories and motivation to tackle larger debts.

☐ **Negotiate Interest Rates:** Explore the possibility of negotiating a lower interest rate with your creditors. A simple phone call can sometimes lead to a reduction in interest rates, making debt repayment more manageable. Creditors are often willing to work with individuals who are committed to meeting their financial obligations.

☐ **Consider Debt Consolidation:** Debt consolidation involves combining multiple debts into one manageable payment. This allows you to optimize your repayment process, reduce interest rates, and simplify financial management. However, it is important to carefully review the terms and conditions of any consolidation plan.

☐ ***Explore Debt Settlement Options***: For people experiencing significant financial hardship, exploring debt settlement options can be a viable strategy. This involves negotiating with your creditors to settle your debt for less than the original amount owed. While it can provide some relief, it may affect your credit score and should be considered carefully.

☐ ***Leverage Windfalls and Bonuses***: Apply windfalls, tax refunds, or work bonuses to pay down debt. Using unexpected financial gains to make substantial payments accelerates the debt repayment process and contributes to your financial control.

☐ ***Seek Professional Guidance:*** If your debt situation seems too complicated, it can be very important to seek professional advice from a credit counselor or financial advisor. These professionals can give you personalized advice, negotiate with creditors on your behalf, and suggest sustainable debt management strategies.

☐ ***Celebrate Milestones along the Way:*** As you progress on the journey towards paying off your debt, celebrate milestones along the way. Acknowledging your accomplishments, whether it's paying off a credit card, meeting a debt reduction goal, or reaching debt-free status, will create positive momentum and increase your commitment to financial freedom.

Remember, paying down debt isn't just a financial endeavor; it's a transformative journey to take control and lay the foundation for future financial success. By implementing these strategies with intention and persistence, you'll pave the way for a better, debt-free future.

Avoiding Common Debt Traps

In the complex tapestry of financial well-being, avoiding the common pitfalls of debt is an essential skill that enables people to build a secure and prosperous future. As your trusted guide on this journey of change, let's look at strategies to avoid these pitfalls and increase your financial resilience.

- **Understanding the Allure of Credit Cards:**

While credit cards are convenient, they can be risky if not handled carefully. The allure of instant gratification and late payments can lead to accumulating high-interest debt. Avoid these pitfalls by using your credit cards wisely, paying balances in full each month, and avoiding unnecessary impulse purchases.

- **Resisting Lifestyle Inflation:**

As your income increases, you are often tempted to upgrade your lifestyle. However, giving in to lifestyle inflation can increase your expenses and lead to debt. Develop a mindset to spend more intentionally, focusing on what you need rather than what you want, increasing your savings, paying down debt, or setting aside profits.

- **Thoughtful Auto Financing:**

Auto loans can be a potential debt trap due to their extended terms and attractive interest rates. Avoid over-committing by researching and negotiating favorable loan terms. To reduce the financial strain associated with owning a car, consider choosing a used car or exploring alternatives such as public transport.

- **Beware of Payday Loans:**

Payday loans, with high interest rates and short repayment periods, often lead to a cycle of debt. Explore alternative financial solutions and emergency funds to meet unexpected expenses, avoiding the quick-fix allure of payday loans.

- **Mindful Student Loan Management:**

Education is an investment in your future, but student loans can be a burden if not managed carefully. Understand your loan terms, research federal repayment programs, and consider refinancing options if feasible. Think of your student loans as a strategic investment rather than a burden.

- **Prudent Mortgage Decisions:**
Owning a home is an important financial goal, but choosing the right mortgage is just as important. Avoid the debt trap by choosing a mortgage that aligns with your financial capabilities. If you prefer regular payments, steer clear of adjustable-rate mortgages and be careful not to borrow more than you can comfortably afford.

- **Cautious Use of Home Equity:**
Home equity can be a valuable financial resource, but if used without careful consideration, it can lead to a debt trap. Use your home equity for essential needs or strategic investments, not as a lifestyle upgrade or quick fix for non-essential expenses.

- **Tempering the Desire for Instant Gratification:**

In a world of instant gratification, the temptation to make impulsive purchases can be overwhelming. Develop a conscious approach to spending and distinguish between wants and needs. Implement a waiting period for significant purchases to allow time for careful review and assessment.

- **Regular Financial Audits:**

Preventive measures are important to avoid debt traps. Regularly assess your financial situation through regular check-ins. Check your budget, track spending patterns, and evaluate your debt-to-income ratio. Early detection allows you to proactively address potential red flags.

- 10. **Seeking Professional Guidance:**

If navigating the financial landscape seems overwhelming, seeking guidance from a financial advisor or consultant can be invaluable. Professionals can provide specific advice, help you create a realistic financial plan, and help you avoid common debt pitfalls.

Avoiding the debt trap is not just a financial strategy; it's a mindset shift that leads to prudent and informed financial decisions. By implementing these strategies with dedication and hard work, you will pave the way to a future where financial pitfalls are minimized and the journey to financial well-being is characterized by stability and empowerment.

Building and Growing Wealth

Investing Basics for Millennials

In the dynamic landscape of personal finance, investing is a powerful tool for millennials to grow their wealth and secure their financial future. As your trusted guide, let's embark on the journey into the fundamentals of investing, helping you understand the challenges and empowering you to make informed strategic decisions on your path to financial growth.

- ***Understanding the Fundamentals:*** Investing involves committing money with the expectation of generating returns over time. This can take many forms, from stocks and bonds to real estate and mutual funds. Understanding these basic concepts is the first step towards becoming a confident and informed investor.

- ***Building a Diverse Portfolio:*** Diversification is an important principle in investing. Instead of putting all your financial eggs in one basket, spread your investments across different asset classes. This limits risk and ensures that the performance of the overall portfolio is not too dependent on the fate of a single investment.

- ***Harnessing the Power of Compound Interest:*** One of the most powerful forces in investing is compound interest. This magical effect allows you to make your money grow not just on the principal but also through accrued interest. Starting early and allowing your investments to compound over time can grow your wealth exponentially.

- **Understanding Risk Tolerance:** Every investor has a unique risk tolerance-the level of risk they are willing to accept. It is important to assess your risk tolerance to determine the right investment mix for your portfolio. This ensures that your investment strategy aligns with your financial goals and emotional comfort.

- **Setting Clear Investment Goals:** Define your investment goals before entering the market. Whether it's saving for a home, funding your education, or saving for retirement, having clear goals can help you develop an investment strategy. Each goal may require a different approach and timeline.

- ***Embracing Long-term Vision:*** Investing is a marathon, not a sprint. Millennials have the advantage of time on their side. Embrace a long-term vision for your investments to help you weather market fluctuations and benefit from compound interest. Patience and consistency are important qualities in the world of investing.

- ***Exploring Different Investment Vehicles:*** Millennials have a variety of investment options available to them. Explore stocks, bonds, index funds, and retirement accounts such as 401(k)s and IRAs. Understanding the characteristics and potential returns of each investment vehicle can help you make strategic choices.

- ***Staying Informed and Educated:*** The investment environment is dynamic and constantly changing. Stay up-to-date with market trends, economic indicators, and new opportunities. Continuing education is a powerful tool that improves your ability to make informed investment decisions.

- ***Utilizing Technology to your Advantage***: Take advantage of technology tools to simplify and improve the investment process. Online platforms, robo-advisors, and investment apps offer accessible avenues that make it easy for millennials to start their investment journey.

- **Seeking Professional Guidance:** If the intricacies of investing seem overwhelming, consider consulting financial advisors. Professionals can provide you with personalized advice, help you define your investment strategy, and help you navigate market challenges with confidence.

Investing, when approached with knowledge and a strategic mindset, can make all the difference in your wealth creation. By embracing these investing fundamentals, millennials can navigate the path to financial growth, achieve their goals, and secure a future of financial stability and prosperity.

Navigating the World of Real Estate and Other Investments

Embarking on the challenging journey of real estate and other investments is like setting sail on a sea of opportunities and challenges. As your experienced guide, let's navigate the complexities of real estate and other investments, exploring strategies to ensure a journey characterized by informed decisions, resilience, and prosperity.

1. Understanding Real Estate as an Investment:

Real estate holds a unique position in the investment world, offering both tangible assets and the potential for long-term appreciation. It's important to understand the basics of real estate as an investment, whether it's residential, commercial, or a real estate investment trust (REIT).

2. Strategic Property Selection:

Choosing the right property is a strategic art. Consider factors such as location, market trends, growth potential, and the general economic environment. Each property should align with your investment goals, whether it's rental income, property appreciation, or a combination of the two.

3. The Role of Diversification:

Diversification goes beyond traditional investments to include real estate. Consider how real estate fits into your overall investment portfolio, balancing it with other assets such as stocks and bonds. Diversification limits risk and enhances the resilience of your investment strategy.

4. Risk Management in Real Estate:

Real estate investments come with their share of risks, from market fluctuations to unexpected real estate expenses. Implement risk management strategies, including due diligence, maintaining an emergency fund for property expenses, and exploring insurance options to protect your investment.

5. Real Estate Financing Strategies:

Navigating real estate often involves financing strategies. Whether it's a mortgage for a primary residence or leveraging other financing options, it's important to understand the intricacies of interest rates, loan terms, and the impact they can have on your overall financial situation.

6. Exploring Alternative Investments:

Explore alternative investments other than real estate. These could be investments in precious metals, cryptocurrencies, or venture capital. Each alternative investment has unique risks and potential rewards, requiring careful consideration and a clear alignment with your financial goals.

7. Staying Informed on Market Trends:

In the dynamic world of investments, staying informed about market trends is a continuous process. Regularly monitor developments in the real estate market, economic indicators, and other investment sectors. With this knowledge, you can make informed decisions and adjust your investment strategy accordingly.

8. Balancing Short-term and Long-term Investments:

Maintaining the right balance between short-term and long-term investments is critical to financial success. Real estate can provide long-term appreciation, while other investments can provide short-term liquidity and returns. Building a balanced portfolio ensures stability and adaptability.

9. Professional Guidance for Complex Decisions:

It is recommended that you seek professional advice when making complex investment decisions. Financial advisors, real estate professionals, and legal experts can provide valuable information, help you navigate the complexities, and ensure that your investment choices are aligned with your overall financial plan.

10. Evaluating your Risk Tolerance:

Understanding your risk tolerance is a key factor in navigating the world of real estate and other investments. Assess your comfort level based on market fluctuations, property management responsibilities, and overall investment volatility. This self-awareness guides your decision-making process.

As you embark on this financial journey, remember that the journey is just as important as the destination. Navigating the world of real estate and other investments requires strategic planning, continuous education, and a resilient mindset. By embracing these principles, you'll set sail toward a future of financial prosperity and a diverse portfolio that can withstand the tides of economic change.

Smart Savings and Spending

Effective Saving Strategies

In the symphony of financial well-being, an effective savings strategy is the keynote that harmonizes the music of your financial journey. As your dedicated guide, let's delve into a comprehensive exploration of strategies that will not only help you build a savings habit but also empower you on the path to lasting financial prosperity.

1. *Cultivating the Savings Mindset:* At the heart of effective saving lies the mindset. Embrace saving as a conscious and intentional action rather than just a thought. Recognize your financial goals and the role savings play in achieving them. This change in mindset lays the foundation for

sustainable and conscious saving habits.

2. *Establishing Clear Financial Goals:* Saving effectively starts with considering your destination. Set specific, achievable financial goals, such as building an emergency fund, saving for a home, or preparing for retirement. Defining these goals provides the motivation and direction you need to navigate your savings journey.

3. *Creating a Realistic Budget:* A realistic budget serves as a compass, guiding your saving efforts. Outline your income, categorize your expenses, and set aside some for savings. A well-prepared budget not only prioritizes savings but also shows clearly where your money is going.

4. *Embracing the 50/30/20 Rule:* The 50/30/20 rule, popularized by financial experts, allocates 50% of your income to needs, 30% to wants, and 20% to savings. This balanced approach provides a systematic yet flexible framework for managing finances, making savings a consistent and meaningful part of your financial plan.

5. *Automated Saving:* Leverage the power of automation to streamline your savings efforts. Set up automatic transfers from your checking account to a designated savings account. This "hands-off" approach makes saving a habit and reduces the temptation to spend before saving.

6. *Windfall Management:* Whether it's a tax refund, a bonus, or an unexpected

gift, windfalls present unique savings opportunities. Instead of being tempted to spend right away, use some of your earnings to save. This proactive approach maximizes the impact of unexpected financial returns on your long-term goals.

7. *Implementing the Cash Envelope System:* For discretionary spending categories, consider the cash envelope system. Allocate a certain amount of money to certain spending categories, such as entertainment or dining out. Once the cash is depleted, it serves as a gentle reminder to prioritize saving for the rest of the month.

8. *Harnessing Technology:* Modern technology offers a variety of tools to improve your savings strategies. Use budgeting apps, savings apps, and

online banking features to track your spending, set savings goals, and get notifications. Technology not only simplifies the process of saving but also provides real-time insights into your financial habits.

9. *Prioritizing High-Interest Debt Repayment*: While saving is important, addressing high-interest debt is equally essential. Prioritize debt repayment to reduce interest payments, freeing up more funds for saving in the long run. This dual strategy provides a holistic approach to financial well-being.

10. *Regularly Reviewing and Adjusting*: The financial landscape is evolving, and so should your savings strategies. Review your budget regularly, reassess your financial goals, and adjust your savings accordingly. This proactive approach

ensures that your savings strategies remain aligned with your ever-changing financial situation.

Effective saving is not just a financial task; it is a holistic approach to improving your financial well-being. By incorporating these strategies into your financial routine, you'll begin a journey where saving becomes not a burden but an intentional and responsible activity that will move you toward a future of financial security and abundance.

Conscious Spending Habits

In the intricate tapestry of financial well-being, conscious spending habits appear as a brush that paints a portrait of conscious living and fiscal empowerment. Let us, as your trusted guide, journey into the realm of conscious spending and explore the profound impact it can have on your finances and overall sense of fulfillment.

- ***Cultivating Financial awareness:*** The key to conscious spending is to practice financial prudence. This means becoming more aware of your spending decisions, understanding the motives behind your purchases, and aligning your expenditures with your values and long-term goals.

- ***Defining your Financial Value:*** Before you spend consciously, take the time to define your financial worth. What is most important to you? Is it experiences, security, or future financial freedom? Being clear about these values provides you with a compass to navigate the vast sea of purchasing options.

- ***Distinguish between Needs and Wants:*** Conscious spending develops through the distinction between wants and needs. While it is important to satisfy your needs, it is equally important to discern when a purchase is based on a genuine necessity rather than buying based on a momentary desire. This judgment is the cornerstone of mindful financial choices.

- **Setting Spending Intentions**: Instead of giving in to impulse spending, set clear intentions before you make purchases. Ask yourself: Does this align with my financial goals? Does it provide lasting value or momentary satisfaction? Setting intentions allows you to make informed choices that align with your overarching objectives.

- **Implementing the 24-hour Rule**: Use the 24-hour rule to avoid impulse spending. If you're faced with a non-urgent purchase, give yourself a

24-hour grace period before completing the transaction. This pause gives you time to reflect, helping you evaluate the necessity and impact on your financial well-being.

- **Embracing Quality over Quantity:** Conscious spending often involves a shift from quantity to quality. Instead of accumulating possessions, focus on purchasing items that provide lasting value and align with your values. This shift not only curtails unnecessary expenses but also fosters a sense of satisfaction with your possessions.

- **Mindful Consumption and Sustainability:** Consider the environmental and social impact of your purchases. Conscious consumption involves choosing products and services that align with sustainability and ethical practices.

This mindful approach not only contributes to a healthier planet but also resonates with an evolving global awareness.

- **Tracking and Analyzing Spending Patterns:** Track and analyze your spending patterns regularly. Utilize budgeting tools, apps, or simple spreadsheets to find out where your money is going. This awareness allows you to identify areas where you can consciously adjust your spending to promote financial growth.

- **Practicing Gratitude for abundance:** An important aspect of conscious spending is cultivating a mindset of gratitude. Realize that every purchase is a choice, and recognize and appreciate the abundance in your life. Gratitude will transform your relationship with money, increase your satisfaction, and reduce your need for mindless consumerism.

- **Budgeting for Joy**: Set aside a portion of your budget for a particularly happy event. Whether it's a special meal, a cultural event, or a weekend getaway, consciously budgeting for pleasure can enrich your life in significant ways by ensuring your spending is aligned with your happiness and well-being.

Mindful spending is not a restrictive practice but a liberating one that allows you to make choices that align with your values and ambitions. By building these mindful spending habits into the fabric of your financial journey, you embark on a path to making every purchase an intentional step toward a future of fulfillment, financial well-being, and a sense of harmony.

Career and Income Growth

Negotiating Salaries and Advancing Your Career

In the complex process of career development, the ability to negotiate salaries is an important and outstanding skill that determines not only financial compensation but also personal and professional growth. As your dedicated guide on this career advancement journey, let's explore the nuanced art of salary negotiation and unlock the doors to a more professional future.

☐ **Understanding your Professional Value:**

The foundation of a successful salary negotiation is a deep understanding of your professional value. Think about your skills, experiences, and the unique contributions you bring to the table. A clear understanding of your worth forms the foundation upon which your negotiation strategies are built.

☐ **Researching Industry Standards:**
Before starting negotiations, conduct thorough research on industry salary standards. Find out the average salary for your role, taking into account factors such as location, experience, and industry trends. This knowledge equips you with a benchmark for fair and competitive negotiations.

☐ **Timing and Tact in Negotiation:**
Timing is an art in negotiations. Ideally, salary discussions should take place after you receive a job offer, but before signing any contracts. Tactfully show your interest in the role and the organization before delving into the negotiation conversation. This strategic

approach sets a positive tone for the discussion.

☐ Crafting a Compelling Case:
Presenting a compelling case is similar to weaving a persuasive narrative. Clearly describe your achievements, skills, and the real value you bring to the organization. Use specific examples of your contributions to demonstrate your impact and justify your request for a higher salary.

☐ Consider the Entire Compensation Package:
Salary negotiations extend beyond the basic figure. Consider the entire compensation package, including benefits, bonuses, and career development opportunities. A holistic approach ensures that your overall package matches your career goals and financial aspirations.

□ **Practicing Assertiveness with Diplomacy:**

Negotiation is a delicate dance that requires assertiveness tempered with diplomacy. Be clear about your expectations and be open to discussion. Instead of treating negotiations from a confrontational standpoint, treat them as a collaborative effort to reach a mutually beneficial agreement.

□ **Anticipating and Addressing Objections:**

Anticipate potential objections and proactively address them in your negotiation strategy. Whether it's budget constraints or the need for additional experience, having well-prepared responses demonstrates insight and a willingness to find common ground.

☐ **Leveraging Additional Benefits:**
If the organization is unable to meet your salary expectations, explore additional benefit options. This may include flexible working arrangements, professional development opportunities, or performance-based bonuses. Strategic negotiation extends beyond the numerical realm, encompassing the overall work experience.

☐ **Seeking Mentorship and Guidance**:
Before entering negotiations, seek mentorship and guidance from experienced professionals in your industry. Learn from their knowledge and experiences, gaining helpful tips for navigating the nuances of salary negotiations. This mentorship provides a supportive foundation for your negotiation endeavors.

☐ **Continual Professional Development:** Career advancement includes a commitment to continuous professional development. Stay informed about industry trends, learn new skills, and actively seek growth opportunities within your organization. A proactive approach to professional development increases overall professional value and establishes a solid foundation for negotiation.

Salary negotiation is more than a transaction; it is a strategic dialogue that shapes the trajectory of your professional journey. By mastering the art of negotiation, you open doors to greater financial gains, personal growth, and a career that aligns with your aspirations. Approach negotiations with confidence, armed with knowledge of your worth, and embark on a transformative journey toward a more rewarding professional future.

Exploring Side Hustles and Additional Income Streams

In the evolving tapestry of personal finance, the notion of side hustles and additional income streams emerges as a vibrant thread, connecting opportunities for financial empowerment and personal fulfillment. As your experienced guide in this quest, let us explore the multi-faceted world of supplementary income, uncovering avenues that not only strengthen your financial standing but also add depth to your professional and personal journey.

- ***Identifying your Passion and Skills:*** The journey into a side hustle often begins with understanding your passions and skills. What activities bring you joy? Where do your talents lie? Identifying these aspects will serve as a compass to guide you toward side hustles that match your true interests and capabilities.

- **Transforming Hobbies into Hustles**: Many successful side hustles stem from personal hobbies and interests. Whether it's photography, writing, crafts, or any other passion, think about how you can transform these hobbies into income-generating activities. Turning something you love into a side hustle adds an element of joy to your quest for extra income.

- **Assessing Market Demand**: While passion is the driving force, assessing market demand is just as important. Research the demand for related products or services to determine the viability of your side hustle. Understanding the market landscape will ensure that your efforts meet customer needs and increase your chances of financial success.

- ***Balancing Time and Energy:*** One of the main challenges when dealing with side hustles is balancing your time and energy effectively. Assess your current commitments, both personal and professional, and carve out dedicated time. Finding the right balance can help you prevent burnout and make your extra income endeavor more sustainable.

- ***Leveraging Online Platforms:*** The digital era offers many online platforms that serve as fertile ground for side hustles. Whether it's freelancing, e-commerce, or content creation, platforms like Upwork, Etsy, or social media offer accessible avenues to showcase your skills and reach a global audience.

- ***Investing in Skill Development***: Side hustles often thrive when supported by a diverse skill set. Invest in your skill development to improve the quality and appeal of your offerings. Online courses, seminars, and mentorship programs can provide valuable information and improve your proficiency in areas relevant to your side hustle.

- ***Exploring Passive Income Streams***: In addition to active side hustles, explore passive income streams that generate income with minimal effort. This may include investments, royalties, or income from automated digital products. Diversifying your income sources contributes to long-term financial stability and resilience.

- ***Networking and Building Connections:*** The power of networking in the world of side hustles should not be underestimated. Connect with your industry or community, attend events, and participate in online forums. Networking opens doors to partnerships, mentorship, and potential opportunities that can increase the success of your side hustle.

- ***Managing Finances Effectively:*** WIth additional sources of income comes the need for effective financial management. Create separate accounts for your side hustle earnings, track expenses, and stay organized with financial records. This disciplined approach will ensure that the extra income contributes positively to your overall financial well-being.

- **Building a Growth Mindset:** Embrace a growth mindset as you navigate the realm of side hustles. See challenges as opportunities to learn and improve. Be flexible and open to evolving your side hustle based on feedback and market dynamics. A growth mindset promotes resilience and ensures that your side hustle remains a dynamic force in your life.

Exploring side hustles and additional income streams is not just a financial strategy; it is a journey of self-discovery, skill development, and potential fulfillment. By approaching this search with intention, passion, and a commitment to continued growth, you embark on a transformative path that not only enriches your financial landscape but also adds another layer of richness to your professional and personal life.

Navigating Financial Challenges

Coping with Economic Uncertainty

In times of ever-changing economic uncertainty, the ability to navigate through turbulence becomes an essential skill. As your empathetic guide through these challenging times, let's explore strategies and thoughtful insights that can help you not only deal with economic uncertainty but also promote stability and growth in the face of unpredictable trends.

1. Cultivating Emotional Resilience:
The first step in coping with economic uncertainty is developing emotional resilience. Acknowledge your feelings of anxiety or stress, and allow yourself to feel them. Emotional resilience doesn't mean suppressing emotions; but about

understanding them and responding with a sense of balance and adaptability.

2. Assessing and Adapting Financial Priorities:

In times of economic uncertainty, it is essential to reassess and adjust your financial priorities. Distinguish between important and non-essential expenses. Create a revised budget that reflects current financial realities, placing emphasis on necessities while temporarily reducing discretionary spending.

3. Building and Strengthening Emergency Funds:

An emergency fund serves as a financial lifeline during times of uncertainty. If possible, make building or strengthening your emergency fund a priority. Having a financial cushion gives you a sense of security and flexibility, allowing you to face unexpected challenges with confidence.

4. Enhancing Financial Literacy:

Empower yourself by becoming financially literate. Understand economic trends, investment options, and the broader financial environment. This knowledge equips you with the tools to make informed decisions and navigate economic uncertainties with a sense of control.

5. Diversifying Income Streams:

Diversifying income streams is a strategic approach to mitigate economic uncertainty. Explore additional sources of income or side hustle that fits your skills and interests. A diversified income portfolio not only strengthens your financial stability, but also improves your ability to adapt to changing economic circumstances.

6. Seeking Professional Financial Advice:

In times of economic uncertainty, professional financial advice can be invaluable. Financial advisors can provide you with personalized insights, recommend investment management strategies, and guide you in making informed decisions to achieve your financial goals.

7. Maintaining Mental and Physical Well-being:

Economic uncertainty often takes a toll on mental and physical well-being. Prioritize self-care practices such as regular exercise, mindfulness, and adequate sleep. A resilient mind and body are better equipped to face challenges and navigate the complexities of uncertain times.

8. Networking and Building Supportive Connections:

Make connections in your professional and personal networks. Share your experiences, insights, and support with others facing similar challenges. Networks foster a sense of community and create a collaborative environment where people can share resources and navigate uncertainty together.

9. Setting Realistic Goals and Milestones:

Set clear short- and long-term goals during times of economic uncertainty. Break down big goals into manageable milestones. Celebrate the small victories along the way, reinforcing a sense of accomplishment and progress even in the face of economic challenges.

10. Embracing a Growth Mindset:

Coping with economic uncertainty is not just about survival; it's an opportunity for growth. Adopt a growth mindset that sees challenges as opportunities to learn and adapt. Treat setbacks as temporary obstacles to personal and financial growth.

Remember, economic uncertainty is a common experience for many people. By approaching these uncertain times with resilience, adaptability, and a proactive mindset, you not only cope with challenges but also lay the foundation for personal and financial growth. Together, we will navigate these turbulent waters, finding strength in our collective ability to face and overcome uncertainty.

Overcoming Unexpected Expenses

Life's journey is often accompanied by unexpected twists and turns, and unforeseen expenses can emerge as a challenging detour on the road to financial well-being. As your empathetic guide through the maze of unexpected costs, we'll look at practical strategies and insights to help you not only overcome sudden financial challenges but also build resilience and fortitude for the unexpected.

- ***Establishing an Emergency Fund:*** Having an emergency fund is a cornerstone of financial stability. This fund acts as a safety net and provides a financial cushion in case unexpected expenses arise. Aim to set aside 3 to 6 months' worth of living expenses as an emergency fund so that you can easily face unexpected financial bumps.

- ***Prioritizing and Budgeting for Contingencies:*** Integrate an emergency budget into your financial planning. Allocate a portion of your monthly budget specifically for unexpected expenses. This proactive approach ensures you always have funds available to meet unexpected expenses without disrupting your overall financial stability.

- **Urgency and impact assessment:** When unexpected expenses arise, assess the urgency and impact of each situation. Distinguish between immediate necessities and less pressing matters. Address important needs first, then allocate resources to manage less urgent costs. This strategic approach helps in the efficient management of financial resources.

- **Negotiating Payment Plans:** In situations where immediate payment is challenging, don't hesitate to negotiate a payment plan with service providers or creditors. Many organizations are willing to work with people facing unexpected financial challenges. Open communication and a proactive approach can lead to mutually beneficial solutions.

- *Tapping into Available Resources*: Explore available resources such as insurance policies, employee benefits, and community support programs. Insurance coverage may mitigate some of the unexpected expenses, and employer benefits such as flexible spending accounts or assistance programs can provide additional support during challenging times.

- ***Seeking Professional Financial Guidance:*** If unexpected expenses feel overwhelming, seek guidance from financial professionals. Financial advisors can provide you with personalized advice, helping you navigate your specific situation and create a plan to overcome current challenges while ensuring your long-term financial goals.

- ***Temporarily Adjusting Non-Essential Spending:*** During periods of unexpected expenses, you may want to consider temporary adjustments to non-essential expenses. This may involve cutting back on discretionary purchases or finding creative ways to reduce expenses. Redirecting funds from non-essential areas allows you to allocate your resources where they are most needed.

- ***Exploring Additional Income Sources:*** Explore additional income opportunities, whether part-time work, freelancing, or temporary gigs. Supplementing your income during tough times can help bridge financial gaps and provide a practical solution to unexpected expenses.

- ***Fostering a Positive Mindset:*** Stay positive even when unexpected expenses arise. View challenges as temporary obstacles in your financial journey rather than insurmountable barriers. A positive mindset not only helps relieve stress but also promotes creativity when it comes to finding solutions to financial challenges.

- ***Learning and Growing from the Experiences:*** Every unexpected expense presents a unique learning opportunity.

Reflect on the experience, evaluate what you could have done differently, and incorporate those lessons into your ongoing financial strategy. Every challenge is a stepping stone to greater financial wisdom and resilience.

Remember, overcoming unexpected expenses is not just a financial task; it is a journey of adaptation, inventiveness, and personal growth. By approaching these challenges with a proactive mindset and strategic planning, you will not only be able to weather the current financial storm, but you will also become stronger, more resilient and better prepared for the unpredictable nature of life's financial journey.

Planning for the Future

Retirement Planning for Millennials

Amid the complex patchwork of financial planning, the concept of retirement may seem like a distant horizon for millennials. However, the journey to financial freedom and a secure retirement begins with careful planning and conscious action. Let's explore the world of retirement planning for millennials and discover strategies to ensure financial security and future fulfillment.

1. Embracing the Power of Time:

One of the unique advantages of millennials is time. Time is a potent ally in the realm of retirement planning, allowing the magic of compounding to work its wonders. By starting early, you can build a solid foundation for retirement by making modest contributions that grow exponentially over time.

2. Setting Clear Retirement Goals:

Define your retirement goals clearly and precisely. Consider the lifestyle you envision, potential travel plans, and any hobbies or passions you wish to pursue. Setting specific goals creates a roadmap for your retirement planning and helps you identify the financial milestones needed to reach them.

3. Leveraging   Employer-Sponsored Retirement Plan:

Make the most of employer-sponsored retirement plans like 401(k)s. These plans often come with employer matching contributions, effectively doubling your savings. At the very least, to take advantage of this valuable benefit, contribute enough to increase your employer's compliance.

4. Exploring Individual Retirement Accounts (IRAs):

Supplement your employer-sponsored plan with Individual Retirement Accounts (IRAs). Traditional IRAs offer tax-deferred growth, while Roth IRAs offer tax-free withdrawals in retirement. Diversifying retirement savings across a variety of accounts increases flexibility and tax efficiency.

5. Balancing Student Loan Repayment and Retirement Savings:

Millennials may face the challenge of balancing student loan repayment and retirement savings. Strive to find a balance that suits your financial priorities. Look into income-driven loan repayment plans and allocate a portion of your income to retirement savings to create a harmonious equilibrium.

6. Adapting to Career Changes and Entrepreneurship:

The gig economy and entrepreneurial ventures characterize the work landscape for many millennials. Adapt your retirement plan to accommodate career changes and periods of self-employment. Look at self-employed retirement accounts, such as a Simplified Employee Pension (SEP) IRA or Solo 401(k).

7. Considering Homeownership in Retirement Plans:

For millennials, home ownership can be an important part of retirement planning. Consider how home ownership fits into your long-term goals and explore ways to pay off your mortgage before retirement. Outright home ownership can significantly reduce living expenses in retirement.

8. Staying Informed about Investment Options:

The investment landscape is evolving, and awareness is essential. Educate yourself about different investment options, including stocks, bonds, and diversified portfolios. Balance risk and return with a variety of investment strategies and optimize your retirement savings for long-term growth.

9. Continuously Reassessing and Adjusting:

Retirement planning is not a static process; it requires constant reassessment and adjustment. Regularly review your retirement goals, income, and investment portfolio. Make the necessary adjustments as life changes, market conditions change, and financial goals change.

10. **Engaging in Open Conversations about Finances:**

Open communication about finances is integral, especially when planning for retirement with your partner or spouse. Engage in honest conversations about your financial goals, expectations, and strategies. Joint planning allows both partners to be on the same page and actively contribute to a shared retirement vision.

Retirement planning for millennials is not just about financial preparation; it's a journey full of self-discovery, aspirations, and building a future that aligns with your unique vision. By approaching retirement planning with intention, making informed decisions, and committing to continuous adaptation, millennials can pave the way to a retirement that reflects not only financial security but also a fulfilling and purposeful life.

Estate Planning and Wealth Transfer

In the tapestry of financial well-being, estate planning is the common thread that weaves together the complex details of one's legacy. Let's examine the profound importance of estate planning and the art of wealth transfer-a journey that transcends the world of finance and delves into the heart of family, values, and lasting impact.

- **Initiating Conversations on Legacy:** Estate planning is more than a legal process; it is an opportunity to start a meaningful conversation about your legacy. Gather your loved ones and have an open discussion about your values, financial aspirations, and the legacy you want to leave behind. These conversations form the foundation upon which your estate plan is built.

- ***Clarifying Personal and Financial Goals:*** Begin the estate planning process by clarifying your personal and financial goals. Consider how you want to live in retirement, the philanthropic causes close to your heart, and the financial security of your loved ones. A clear understanding of your goals is a guide to creating a comprehensive estate plan.

- ***Drafting a Will and Testament:*** A will is the cornerstone of estate planning, outlining how your assets will be distributed after your death. Be thorough in detailing your wishes, appointing an executor, and considering guardianship for dependents if necessary. Update your will regularly to reflect changes in your life and your changing financial circumstances.

- **Trusts as Strategic Tools:** Trusts offer a strategic approach to wealth transfer. They provide flexibility, control, and privacy in distributing assets. Explore options such as revocable living trusts, irrevocable trusts, or special needs trusts, structuring your trust to fit your specific financial and family objectives.

- **Maximizing Tax Efficiency:** Estate planning involves navigating tax implications to maximize the transfer of wealth to your heirs. Work with financial and legal experts to implement strategies that minimize estate taxes. Take advantage of tools like the lifetime gift tax exemption and consider the impacts of inheritance taxes on your estate.

- **Beneficiary Designations and Asset Titling:** Review and update beneficiary designations in accounts such as life insurance policies, retirement accounts, and investment accounts. Align asset titling with your estate plan to ensure a smooth transfer of assets to your designated heirs. Consistency between beneficiary designations and legal documentation is important.

- ***Powers of Attorney and Healthcare Directives***: Beyond asset allocation, estate planning also includes healthcare and disability financial decisions. Establish a power of attorney for your financial affairs and health care directives, giving trusted individuals the authority to make decisions on your behalf if needed.

- ***Philanthropy and Charitable Giving***: For those with a philanthropic spirit, estate planning provides an opportunity to support charitable causes. Consider setting up charitable trusts or foundations, or including charitable bequests in your will. Combine philanthropy and legacy to make a positive impact in the areas you care about.

- **Continual Review and Adjustments**: Estate planning is not a one-time event; it requires continuous evaluation and adjustments. Review your estate plan regularly to take into account changes in your life, new assets, or changes in financial goals. An adaptable estate plan ensures a dynamic representation of your evolving legacy.
- **Guiding the Next Generation**: Use estate planning as an opportunity to pass financial wisdom on to the next generation. Consider organizing a financial education plan, mentorship

programs, or establishing family meetings to discuss the responsibilities and values associated with wealth transfer. Guiding the next generation ensures a legacy beyond monetary assets.

Estate planning and wealth transfer are profound acts of financial stewardship and love for those you care about. By approaching this process with intention, open communication, and a commitment to creating a legacy that aligns with your values, you embark on a journey that transcends generations, a journey where your financial wisdom and the essence of who you are enduring serve as a lasting legacy for those you hold dear.

Thriving in the Modern Financial Landscape

Embracing Technological Tools for Financial Success

In the dynamic landscape of personal finance, the integration of technological tools has emerged as a transformative force, providing a wealth of resources to support individuals' financial success. As your practical guide to financial well-being, let's explore the importance of using technological tools and how these tools can be a valuable asset on your path to financial wellness.

- ☐ *Budgeting Apps for Financial Clarity:* The foundation of financial success lies in clear budgeting. Modern budgeting apps, such as Mint, YNAB, or

PocketGuard, provide real-time information on your spending habits, categorize your expenses, and offer personalized budget recommendations. These tools will help you make informed decisions and develop a disciplined approach to managing your finances.

☐ ***Investment Platforms for Wealth Growth:*** Investing is the cornerstone of financial success, and technological tools have democratized access to the world of investing. Platforms like Robinhood, Acorns, or Betterment make investing easy, offering features such as automated portfolio management, share participation, and educational resources to guide your investment decisions.

☐ ***Financial Aggregators for Holistic Views:*** It's important to understand your complete financial picture. Financial aggregators like Personal Capital or Wealthfront aggregate your financial accounts, providing a holistic view of your net worth, investments, and liabilities. This comprehensive perspective helps you make informed decisions and strategically plan for long-term financial success.

☐ ***Automation for Seamless Savings:*** Technology enables seamless automation of savings and deposits into investment accounts. Set up automatic payday transfers to your savings or investment accounts. This automation ensures consistent contributions and encourages structured saving habits without constant manual intervention.

☐ ***Credit Score Monitoring for Financial Health:*** Your credit score is an important aspect of your financial well-being. Check your credit score regularly using tools like Credit Karma or Experian. Understanding your credit score and the factors influencing it can help you make strategic decisions that will have a positive impact on your overall financial health.

☐ ***Financial Planning Software for Goal Achievement:*** Achieving financial goals requires strategic planning. Financial planning software like eMoney or Personal Capital makes it easy to set goals, analyze scenarios, and create retirement plans. These tools will help you envision your financial future and make informed decisions that match your aspirations.

☐ **Cryptocurrency Platforms for Diversification:** As digital assets become more popular, you may want to consider a cryptocurrency investment technology platform. Platforms like Coinbase or Gemini provide an easy interface to buy, sell and manage cryptocurrencies. Although volatile, investing in cryptocurrencies offers a potential opportunity for diversification.

☐ **E-learning Platforms for Financial Literacy:** Continuous learning is an essential part of financial success. E-learning platforms like Khan Academy, Udemy, or Coursera offer courses on personal finance, investing, and related topics. Use these platforms to improve your financial literacy and gain insights to make informed financial decisions.

☐ ***Digital Wallet for Convenient Transactions:*** Digital wallets such as Apple Pay, Google Pay, or PayPal offer a convenient and secure way to transact. From shopping to sharing bills with friends, use these tools to streamline your everyday financial activities. Digital wallets provide efficiency and security in the digital age.

☐ ***Cybersecurity Measures for Protection:*** As you embrace technological tools, prioritize cybersecurity. Use password managers, enable two-factor authentication, and stay vigilant for phishing attempts. Protecting your financial information is extremely important, ensuring that your path to financial success remains safe and secure.

Using technological tools for financial success is more than just a modern convenience; it is a strategic choice that improves your ability to handle the complexities of personal finance. By incorporating these tools into your financial toolkit, you begin your journey where technology becomes your ally, empowering you to achieve your financial goals with clarity, efficiency, and informed decision-making.

Adapting to Changing Economic Trends

In an ever-evolving global economy, the ability to adapt to changing economic trends becomes a critical skill—a financial navigation skill that requires persistence, foresight, and a commitment to continuous learning. As your experienced guide through the currents of economic transformation, we will look at the strategies and insights that can help you not only weather the changes but also thrive amidst the changing economic landscape.

1. Cultivating Financial Agility:
Adapting to changing economic trends requires developing financial agility. Be open to adjusting your financial strategy, embracing new opportunities, and reevaluating existing plans. An agile and flexible approach allows us to respond effectively to the dynamic nature of the economic environment.

2. Continuous Learning and Skills Development:
The pace of economic change is often linked to advances in technology and industry practices. Keep learning to keep up with new trends. Acquire new skills relevant to the evolving job market, maintaining a valuable

and adaptable asset in the face of economic change.

3. *Diversification of Income Streams:*

Economic trends can affect industries and job sectors in a variety of ways. Increase your financial stability by diversifying your income streams. Discover side hustles, freelancing, or investment opportunities that fit new trends and provide alternative sources of income in a dynamic economy.

4. *Building a Robust Emergency Fund:*

An emergency fund serves as a financial buffer during times of economic uncertainty. Make sure your emergency fund is enough to cover several months of essential living expenses. This financial cushion provides stability and peace of mind when unexpected financial difficulties arise.

5. Strategic Budgeting for Flexibility:

Plan your budget with flexibility in mind. Allocate resources to both essential and discretionary expenses, leaving room for adjustment based on economic conditions. A strategic budget gives you the flexibility you need to effectively manage fluctuating income and expenses.

6. Networking and Professional Connections:

Networking is a valuable asset in times of economic change. Develop and expand professional relationships within your industry and beyond. Networking provides insight into industry trends, potential opportunities, and a support system for professionals navigating similar economic landscapes.

7. Anticipating Industry Trends:

Stay ahead of the curve by anticipating industry trends. Research and analyze the trajectory of your industry, identifying potential changes in demand, technology, or customer preferences. By proactively anticipating, you can strategically position yourself and adapt your skills to emerging opportunities.

8. Debt Management and Financial Resilience:

Effective debt management becomes important in times of economic volatility. Minimize high-interest debt and prioritize paying off existing loans. Financial stability ensures that debt obligations do not become overwhelming during periods of economic uncertainty.

9. Strategic Investments and Portfolio Diversification:

Review and adjust your investment portfolio in response to changing economic trends. Spread your risk by diversifying your investments across different asset classes. Strategic investments aligned with emerging opportunities contribute to the long-term growth of your financial portfolio.

10. Emotional Resilience and Stress Management:

Adapting to changing economic trends can be emotionally taxing. Develop emotional stability and practice stress management techniques. Maintain a positive mindset, seek support from your network, and engage in activities that promote your well-being. Emotional stability is the cornerstone of effective adaptation.

Adapting to changing economic trends is not just a financial task; it is a journey of personal and professional growth. By approaching these changes with a willingness to adapt, a commitment to learning, and strategic financial planning, you position yourself not as a passive observer but as an active participant in shaping your financial future in an ever-changing economic landscape.

Conclusion

Reflecting on Progress

In the journey of personal development, the art of reflection stands as a powerful compass, guiding people through the complex landscape of development and self-discovery. As your experienced personal growth coach, I will explore the meaning of reflective practice and unlock its transformative potential to create a life of purpose and fulfillment.

1. **The Mirror of Self-Awareness**: Reflection serves as a mirror, providing insight into the depth of self-awareness. Take time to pause and ponder, allowing your thoughts to explore the pathways of your experiences, choices, and emotions. This self-awareness is the foundation

upon which meaningful progress is built.

2. **Recognizing Achievements and Milestones:** In the hustle and bustle of everyday life, it can be easy to overlook the achievements and milestones that commemorate your journey. Reflection allows us to celebrate accomplishments, both big and small. Recognize the steps you've taken, the goals you've reached, and the obstacles you've overcome. This recognition increases motivation and bolsters your sense of accomplishment.

3. **Learning from Challenges and Setbacks: Life's** journey is adorned with challenges and setbacks, each presenting an opportunity for growth. Reflect on the challenges you faced and explore the lessons you learned from

them. What insights did you gain? How have these experiences strengthened your resilience and problem-solving skills? Embrace setbacks as a stepping stone to a more resilient version of yourself.

4. **Aligning Actions with Values:** Reflective practices reveal the alignment (or misalignment) between your actions and your core values. Do your everyday choices reflect the values that are most important to you? This self-awareness guides intentional decision-making and promotes a life of authenticity and purpose.

5. **Evolving Perspectives and Priorities:** As you reflect on your journey, observe the changes in your perspective and priorities. What was once important may have changed with time and

experience. Embrace the changing nature of your priorities, allowing them to adapt in alignment with your ever-evolving understanding of what brings meaning and fulfillment to your life.

6. **Cultivating Gratitude and Positivity:** Reflection provides a space to cultivate gratitude and positivity. Count the moments, relationships and experiences for which you are grateful. This practice promotes a positive mindset, and strengthens your awareness in the abundance that surrounds you, even in the midst of life's challenges.

7. **Navigating Future Aspirations:** Consider reflection as an exploratory tool to identify your future aspirations. What are your dreams and goals? How

do your past experiences shape your future aspirations? Reflection provides clarity and helps you set meaningful intentional goals that align with your evolving vision of a life of purpose and fulfillment.

8. **Deepening Interpersonal Connections:** Reflection goes beyond the individual and includes interpersonal dynamics. Think about your relationships and connections. How have they grown, transformed, or perhaps faced challenges? Reflecting on your relationships promotes deeper understanding and empathy, creating healthy and meaningful relationships.

9. **Balancing Self-compassion and Accountability:** Threads of self-compassion, along with a sense of responsibility, are woven into the

tapestry of reflection. Accept your flaws with kindness, recognizing that growth comes with both breakthroughs and setbacks. Simultaneously, hold yourself accountable for the choices you make that align with your aspirations, encouraging a balanced and constructive approach to personal development.

10. **Creating a Vision for the Future:** Finally, reflection serves as a compass for crafting a vision for the future. Visualize who you want to become as you navigate the landscape of progress. What steps can you take to align your actions with this vision? Reflection provides the clarity and understanding needed to pave the way to a more purposeful and fulfilling future.

In the art of reflecting on progress, embark on a transformational journey, a journey that combines self-awareness, gratitude, and intentional living to create a life rich in meaning and fulfillment. Embrace the reflective process with curiosity and openness, for within it lies the key that unlocks the door to your most authentic and flourishing self.

Wealthy Habits